Penny Pinching Mama
500 Ways I Lived On $500 A Month

By
Jill Cooper

Book cover design by Amy Bleser

Visit us on the Web!
www.LivingOnADime.com

E-mail
editor@livingonadime.com

1

Would you like to learn how to save over $7000 in one year?

Simply go to www.LivingOnaDime.com and sign up for the free weekly newsletter. You'll receive valuable money-saving tips that work, from the authors of this book.

Jill Cooper and Tawra Kellam are a mother daughter team who learned to live in difficult financial circumstances at a time in life when money was always in short supply. Living in a situation where they had to choose between one necessity and another really helped them gain a new perspective about the value of things. It also helped them make distinctions between needs and desires. Their goal is to educate people about better ways to handle money in the hope that the people they touch can live more fulfilled and less stressful lives.

As a single mother of two, *Jill Cooper* started her own business without any capital and paid off $35,000 debt in 5 years on $1,000 a month income.

She then raised two teenagers alone on $500 a month income after becoming disabled with Chronic Fatigue Syndrome.

For her entire life, *Tawra Kellam* has lived the frugal lifestyle. Her mother's determination to persevere through extraordinarily difficult financial circumstances is the basis of Tawra's frugal thinking.

Tawra, her husband and 4 children live in Colorado. In five years, they paid off $20,000 personal debt on an average income of $22,000 per year.

2

Table of Contents

Introduction

I have been asked over and over for practical tips and ideas that explain how I managed to live on $1,000 a month and pay off $35,000 debt in five years.

At the time I earned $12,000 a year. My two children and I lived off of $5,000, and the other $7,000 I put toward paying off debts and my house. After I paid off my debts and house, I became ill with Chronic Fatigue Syndrome and then had to go on disability, I received $500 a month and raised two teenagers.

I have hesitated up to now to give exact details of how I did that only because I was afraid I would scare people off. What I had to do took a lot of hard work, was not easy, and there were few options. I had to find ways to feed, clothe, and shelter my children with only the cash I had in my hand.

There were no credit cards to use at that time or loans I could get. If there was no food left and I had only $2, then I had to figure out ways to make that stretch for three meals the next day.

I really don't think most people today know what it means to be truly destitute. I realized this once again the other day when a reporter asked me how my children and I dealt with the idea of "keeping up with the Joneses." I sat there gaping at her for a few minutes because I thought, "She doesn't have a clue. The Joneses are the least of my problems."

After working 14 to 16 hours a day just to make enough for

food and to keep an inexpensive roof over our heads I was too exhausted to worry about what others thought.

I did not have the luxury of using what little energy I had to indulge in silly negative emotions or self pity. Most of the debt I had had been incurred by my husband while we were separated, but I meant my wedding vows, for better or worse, for richer or poorer. It didn't matter how right or wrong it was or unfair it all was. It was my responsibility.

Besides, I was so grateful to have food to eat, a roof over our heads (even if it did leak), and a car that would actually start most times it didn't matter what kind of house or car it was, how new they were or whether or not I was keeping up with the "Joneses".

The bottom line is to stop dragging yourself down with negative emotions and excuses, accept your responsibilities and with God's help start taking care of them one step at a time.

Don't get overwhelmed!

Everyone's situation and family are different. Some may need just one or two ideas to help them out. Others may need to do all of these things the way I did. These are the things I did to live on $5,000 a year. Use what you can for your family and remember a couple of things:

    1. **Start slowly.** Pick one or two simple things to do at first. After you have mastered those, add another one or two. Try not to overwhelm yourself and remember, if you only do

one thing, you are still farther along than when you started.

2. **These are just ideas and things that I did personally.** If your first thought is "This won't work for my family, so I'll just not try," think again. Maybe you can change or adapt the idea so it *will* work for you.

3. **Get rid of any emotions that are tied up with money.** Stop allowing it to be a god in your life and control you. It is a *thing* and you need to control *it*. I don't care what the rest of the world or other people think. If they are all going to jump off a cliff, then should you jump too? That pretty much is what the rest of the world is doing as far as their money and debt go.

Don't Shop.

NO! NONE! DON'T! And if I didn't make myself clear enough **"Don't go shopping!"** Going shopping (even to window shop) for someone with credit card debt makes as much sense as a recovering alcoholic going each evening to his favorite bar and sitting to watch the people drink. I don't know about you, but I have enough trouble not falling into temptation when I'm *not* near it, let alone putting myself right in the middle of it.

I have only been to a shopping mall *one time* in almost 20 years. Even if I had the money, I'm not sure that I would go to a mall just because it is so stress-free wearing clothes from garage sales and thrift stores. I don't have to worry if I stain a blouse when I spent only $.50 on it. I don't have to have my closet packed with fat and skinny clothes either. If I gain or lose weight, I can replace my entire wardrobe for a season for $25.

I don't look frumpy either. When I'm sitting in a crowded room, I really look no different than the other people who paid tons of money for their outfits. Well, maybe I do a little. I sit with a smile on my face looking relaxed and enjoying myself because I'm not stressed over my money. Some of them tend to look more stressed and sober because they are trying to figure out how to pay for that $300 outfit they are wearing.

There were times when I couldn't even allow myself to go to garage sales. Not only didn't I have money to spend, but I even had to save my gas.

I Bartered As Much As I Could.

Though I have learned many skills and how to do a lot of things over the years that I never imagined I could do, there have been a few things I just haven't seemed to master, so I have learned how to barter. Bartering is simple. **Just Ask.** I have been told 9 times out of 10 "yes."

One of those things I bartered for was haircuts. I couldn't even cut my daughter's bangs, so I bartered to have them done. I can't imagine how much money I've saved just because I asked. Here are many examples of how we have saved money by bartering.

~**I found a woman who was a hairdresser but hated ironing.** I did her ironing and in exchange, she gave us haircuts.

~At one point I couldn't mow my yard, so I traded having my yard mowed for homemade cookies and cinnamon rolls.

~I have traded a plate of cookies for a bouquet of fresh flowers, and books for a massage to help my daughter's fibromyalgia.

~My daughter had a large garden when she was single. She exchanged produce with a local restaurant for meals on the days when she was too sick to cook.

~When I started my business and couldn't pay my old production manager, he was willing to work for me in exchange for piano parts I had.

~My son is a computer wiz. He fixes his father-in-law's computers, and in exchange, his father-in-law does their plumbing.

~If you don't have a green thumb but your neighbor does, then offer to rake leaves or shovel snow off their sidewalk in exchange for some bouquets of flowers in the summer.

~Do you love crocheted things but can't crochet? Then offer to walk an older neighbor's dog in exchange for some doilies.

~Couldn't use a hammer or saw if your life depended on it? Then find out something that a handyman friend needs and offer to help him (or her) with that in exchange for some handyman work.

You don't always have to barter *skills*. You can also barter *things*. For example, I have traded this great book that I love and have a ton of copies of called Dining on a Dime ☺ for other things like books, cute craft things I've seen at craft shows, Mary Kay make-up, and Pampered Chef items.

Here are a couple of last thoughts on bartering. First, once you get started, you are going to want to barter all the time, but don't forget there are times that we should use our skills for others without a thought of what they can do for us in return.

Second, the up-side to that is that there are times when we want to just help someone, but it may hurt their pride or make them feel uncomfortably dependent on us. Bartering is a good way to help with that. An example of this would be an elderly woman who can't get out to get her groceries. You would be more than willing to just do it for her, but she hates to be dependent on anyone. If you ask her to crochet you some doilies, teach you a new skill, or give you some flowers from her garden in exchange for getting her groceries, then you are helping her not feel like a charity case, and the reality is that she *isn't* a charity case because you would love to have the doilies to spruce up your home but can't afford them.

I couldn't fix your brakes, so I made your horn LOUDER!

Grocery Savings

David, Jill and Tawra eating Christmas Dinner at home.

We drank nothing but water. No coffee (and I love my coffee), tea, pop, or juice. When we did have juice, we only had one serving--the amount to fulfill our nutritional requirement for the day.

I carefully regulated what we ate and the size portions we had. For example, we would have one serving of meat. That didn't mean a large serving either but one chicken leg or thigh, one piece of roast beef, etc.

I carefully studied and had down to a science exactly how much of each food group we needed for each meal. That was what I served, no more, no less. I know this may seem a bit harsh and restrictive but I had no choice. If I didn't regulate our food each day like that, it would mean going without the next day.

The odd thing was we really didn't seem to be hungry for more. I think because we were eating such well-balanced meals and getting all the vitamins and minerals we needed, **our bodies were very satisfied, and we didn't have a lot of cravings.**

Now granted, if the kids ever said they were still hungry, I would fix things like large bowls of popcorn, cinnamon toast, or I'd give them another piece of fruit. I really think **we were healthier at those times in our lives** than at any other time, which was a good thing because I had no medical insurance most of the time.

I tried not to have leftovers. I didn't cook huge amounts of food. I knew one medium potato per person was plenty, 1/2 of a potato for a small child. I would fix 1/2 of a sandwich for my young children. If they were still hungry, then they could get another 1/2. They were always given a 1/2 of a piece of fruit or popsicle or glass of milk to start.

When I did have leftovers, I always used up every bit of them.

I stretched food as far as I could. Nothing was wasted. I would make a pot roast stretch into 3-5 meals. I would first cook it and serve it with mashed potatoes and gravy plus side dishes.

Then for the next meal, I cut up small pieces of beef and mixed them with the leftover gravy for hot roast beef sandwiches. Then I shredded some more of the meat, and we had bar-b-que sandwiches. Next I added bouillon cubes to the handful or two of remaining meat and made beef and noodles. Finally, I then took the bone and boiled it for veggie soup.

I did the same things with chicken, turkey, and ham, cooking them for a main meal, then cubing and using the meat in casseroles or with noodles, and last of all, always boiling the bones for soup. In the case of the ham, I could use the bone later for ham and beans.

By using the meat in casseroles, with noodles, or with gravy, I could stretch it much farther. Also if a recipe called for a pound of something like hamburger, I could very easily use only a *half* pound, and no one would know the difference. The same went for chicken. Some noodle or casserole recipes call for a whole cooked chicken. I would use one quarter to one half that amount.

When making chocolate chip cookies, I used a quarter or

half the bag of chocolate chips instead of a full bag.

I regularly shopped the discounted bread, meat, and dairy sections. My daughter gets milk for $1 a gallon. It doesn't expire for a week! Meat has a *sell by* date, and then they have to sell it or throw it away. That is NOT the same as a *use by* date. Meat can still be used 3-4 days after the sell by date. If you don't need to use it right away, just freeze it.

I won't go into more detail on food because I have all those ideas in our cookbook ***Dining on a Dime***, which can be found at **www.LivingOnADime.com**

Ways to Handle Stress

Jam tiny marshmallows up your nose and try to sneeze them out.

Start a cereal box collection

Smear yourself with caramel and make popcorn with the lid off.

Cleaning Supplies

Tawra "helping" clean up the remodeling mess.

I get a lot of my cleaning products at our Hazardous Waste Recycling Center for free.

You really don't need that much for cleaning. I personally have on hand:

> **Comet -** stubborn stains, in my toilet bowl
>
> **Bleach -** disinfectant
>
> **Dow Foaming bath cleaner -** I do use it in the bathroom, but I mostly use it for degreasing in the kitchen.
>
> **Vinegar or rubbing alcohol -** These are good for windows, mirrors, or anything glass and are great degreasers. I don't use these that often because unless I have a real dirty job, I find that just a damp cloth followed by a dry cloth works just fine.
>
> **Pledge -** for dusting. If you can't buy that, then use a very slightly damp rag.
>
> **Ammonia -** for mopping my floors

Always spray the cleaning product on your rag and not on the item you are cleaning. Not only do you save on product, but also time spent trying to wipe all the product off.

I didn't have a dishwasher most of the time, so I didn't buy things like dishwasher detergent.

Toilet Paper - I buy expensive toilet paper but carefully fold it when I use it and don't wad it. Wadding causes you to use 2-3 times as much as you need. (Talk about every part of your life being an open book!). Teach your children to fold and not wad their toilet paper. This also saves on clogged toilets and plumbing problems. An ounce of prevention is worth a pound of cure!

Plastic Bags - Oddly enough I don't wash my bags out a lot. I do however reuse them. For example, I had my children leave their sandwich bags in their lunch boxes. Then the next day I would reuse the ones that had only bread crumbs or cookie crumbs in them.

I used plastic containers when possible instead of sandwich bags.

I would use plastic bags that I brought my fruit home in from the grocery store to cover plates of cookies, sandwiches, etc.

Paper Towels - I used rags, dishrags, and towels instead of paper towels. **I used about 4 rolls of paper towels a year when my kids were young.** I used terry cloth tablecloths that caught any spills made at the table, which helped save on rags or paper towels.

To prevent cross contamination, I used dish rags but always with hot soapy water and/or bleach to wash dishes and wipe counters. For really bad messes, I used a rag and then just throw it away the way others use paper towels. Rags can be made by cutting up old t-shirts, sheets, or towels.

Trash Bags - I have only bought trash bags once in my life and then they weren't to use for trash. Most of the time I use brown paper sacks. I had a garbage disposal, so any gooey or wet things usually went down the drain. Once in awhile if I had something wet or sticky that I didn't want to put down the sink, I just tossed it in a plastic grocery bag and then put it in the trash.

Just stop being so wasteful. When you start being more careful with what you buy, and use up what you do have, then you will have less trash, which means having to use fewer trash bags. I was always aware and watched how much I would use of anything, so I wasted as little as possible. So often people grab for a paper towel, and they take five or six in a wad when one or two towels would have been enough. Watch for wastefulness in all areas of your life.

Grooming

David and Tawra with her first home perm.

I spent very little money on my grooming needs, such as haircuts, nails, etc. I have often been asked, **"How did you manage to feel good about yourself and not get depressed?"** I found out by accident that when you are trying to be responsible about your bills and money, trying to do what is right and act with integrity, then you feel good about yourself. My self-esteem was not wrapped up in an expensive haircut or nails.

My self-confidence came from within and not from outward appearances. It's a good and righteous pride in yourself and not a false pride. It's a better feeling than when you are trying to ward off the bill collectors.

Now that doesn't mean you have to look like a slob if you don't have money. Oddly enough, unless people knew me very well, they didn't know I had very little money. I wore name brand clothes that were clean and ironed, my hair in an updated style even when I couldn't always get it cut, and I kept my shoes clean and polished.

I learned to stretch all of my toiletries as far as possible, even cutting open containers to get the last little bit.

I had only four kinds of make up -- foundation, blush, mascara, and lipstick. I used these items sparingly and not at all on the days when I would be staying home. I also asked for these things as birthday or Christmas gifts when I needed them.

One container of foundation, blush, etc., would often last me for 2-3 years. I know all about how you need to throw this stuff out after 6 months because of bacteria, but I had no choice. It was either toss it and do without or use it and hope the army of bacteria didn't eat a hole in my face.

I sold make up for many years and never really had a problem with anyone who used old make up except once, and the lady had her make up almost 10 years and the worst thing that happened was her face had started breaking out. As soon as she started some new make up, her face cleared up. If your face is acting normal, then just keep using your old make up.

Use common sense. If you start getting unusual rashes, etc., then change your make up and see if that helps. Of course, the exception to the rule is if you ever have an eye infection, then always change your eye make up.

You need to get rid of the spirit of fear. Use common sense and make do. There may be times when things happen, like your face breaking out because of old make up. So often we function out of fear instead of common sense. Watch the commercial world and notice how often they play on your sense of fear. If you don't buy this or that, then you aren't going to be loved, you won't look sexy, or your children will hate you. And one of the greatest fears of all, what will people think?

Sometimes you have to get rid of the fear, step out and take a chance. Besides, I'm sorry, but **if you don't have the money, you don't have the money.** If my mascara is going to give me eyeball rot because I didn't throw it out when the company who wants to sell me more make up said to, well so be it. I had two choices, use old make up or don't use anything. I chose to use it. (By the way, I didn't get eyeball rot.)

For a long time I never had my hair done professionally.
I couldn't afford to have it cut, so I always wore it long. I also
made sure that I kept it in an updated style.

I cut back on how many times a week I washed my hair.
I washed it every two to three days instead of every day.
Even though I had extremely oily hair, I found that
shampooing once instead of twice worked just as well.

I did my own manicures and pedicures. I would
sometimes buy one bottle of polish and only one, which
would last me a long time. At times I couldn't even buy
polish, so I kept my nails neatly trimmed and clean and I still
looked nice.

**I didn't buy bubble bath, bath wash, powders, or
perfumes.** Just soap. Sometimes I received these things as
gifts, so I never seemed to have to do without.

I found out when using face lotions and creams that they are
like fertilizer that you use on your yard. **When they say to
use a small amount, they mean it.**

With fertilizer, if you use too much, you can mess up the
whole purpose of fertilizer and kill your grass -- the less you
use of it, the better it works. Remember that when using your
creams and lotions too. This is one case where more is not
always better.

**I didn't buy things like special hairbrushes or hair
accessories.** I even had my blow dryer or curling iron die on
me but I made do without.

As unbelievable as it seems, there was a time in history

where they didn't have blow dryers and curling irons. If I was in a hurry, I would do things like dry my hair in front of a fan or heater, and in Kansas many days I could go out and the wind would blow it dry instantly. If my curling iron died, I would drag out my old fashioned curlers. I have even used rags before.

I either did without or made do with what I had. My purse once died on me, so I started just carrying my wallet. I who carried everything but the kitchen sink in my purse (well sometimes I *did* have parts from the kitchen sink in there because I spent 20 years remodeling my house) learned how to make do with only my wallet. Another time I needed a purse and I saw a fur one for $100 on TV, so I made one for myself out of an old piece of fur I had laying around.

Why Ask Why?

Why is it that no matter what color bubble bath you use, the bubbles are always white?

Clothes/Laundry

Jill made Tawra's Easter dress out of an old housecoat.

Demystifying the Great Laundry Dilemma

Most adults buy clothes just because they want something new and different, not because they really need them. There should be no reason to buy clothes for adult members of the family during a financial crisis. The only exception would be if a suit or special clothes for work is needed. Even then, try to borrow a suit or go to a thrift store to buy one.

When I needed dress-up clothes, I used my basic black skirt, 2-3 blouses, changed my jewelry, and used scarves so it seemed like I had more outfits than I really did.

Once again, I didn't have the luxury to worry about what other people thought of me wearing the same outfit over and over. You know what I found out, though? Most people couldn't care less what I was wearing.

This may seem like a small thing, but I think it is important. When possible, keep your clothing neat and tidy. Keep your shoes shined or in the case of tennis shoes, washed. Iron your clothes. Even a worn flannel shirt, T-shirt, or pair of jeans look better when ironed. It helps you to have more self-confidence and to feel better about yourself when you know you are looking your best.

Look through your closet thoroughly and make sure there isn't something in there that you could maybe revamp. Do you perhaps have an outdated dress that would look good if you just pulled a ruffle off or pulled up the hem?

If you really need something to wear, go to a garage sale or thrift store.

Take care of the clothes you do have. If you wear something once and it isn't dirty, then wear it again before you wash it. Of course, we need to wear clean underwear and socks every day. I do recommend that. I'm not a total barbarian. ☺

Don't use the dryer. I never used my dryer when I couldn't afford it. Not only did it save on electricity, but it saved on wear and tear on my family's clothes. That is why the elastic keeps stretching out of everything and you have to keep replacing them.

If you must use your dryer, then at least hang the socks and underwear on a drying rack, radiator, shower curtain rod, or something like that. I had hot water radiators for heat. I dried my clothes on them a lot.

You will, of course, have to buy children's clothes because of wear and tear and out growing things. Children don't have to have a closet packed full of clothes, though.

My kids were so thankful to even have a pair of jeans to wear and not go naked that it really didn't matter to them that they weren't name brand items.

Buy kids clothes at garage sales or thrift stores.

Exchange clothes with friends and family.

Accept all hand-me-downs. Use what you can and pass the rest on to someone else.

Make do with what you have. If your child's long-sleeved shirt is getting too short, then cut off the sleeves for a short-sleeved shirt. Turn T-shirts into tank tops. My granddaughter seems to only outgrow her pants in length and not around the waist, so my daughter-in-law cut her pants off and made capris and then they can be cut into shorts.

If pants or jeans get a tear in the knee, then for a little girl **put a cute heart or flower appliqué or the hole.** You could, of course, cut them off for shorts too.

If you can't sew, you can now get fabric glue or fusible web. Any person at a fabric store can show what that is.

If your daughter gets a hole in her shirt, mend it and then attach a cute button, heart, or flower patch on it. If I'm not giving an article of clothing away, **I cut off all the buttons and anything cute on it before I use it for a rag.** That way I have a supply of things when I need a patch.

Take hems up and down. Sew on missing buttons. Mend tears. If your little boys lose a button on the front of a shirt and you can't find one to match, then use the button at the top of the shirt by the neck to replace it. Most guys don't button that top button anyway, so it won't be noticed. I do this with my button-down shirts too. I very rarely button the cuff on my long-sleeved shirts because I roll up the sleeves, so I also use the button from the cuff on those shirts when I need to.

If winter is coming and your daughter has 10 perfectly good short-sleeved shirts, then instead of buying 5-6 winter shirts, buy 1-2 neutral cardigan sweaters for her to wear over her T-shirts.

The entire sole of my son's shoe came off once. I didn't have money to get him a new pair. We had to make do, so I hot glued it back together. Now granted, I had to re-glue it back together every few days, but it lasted long enough until I could buy him a new pair. Now they sell glue made just for gluing the soles onto shoes.

Let the kids go barefoot as much as possible in the summer or just buy inexpensive sandals.

Don't buy kids new school clothes.

We have been brainwashed into thinking we need to buy our kids an entire new wardrobe every August or September, but I never bought my kids school clothes. I always wondered if everyone's kids went naked all summer long and then all of a sudden they needed clothes two weeks before school.

My children don't seem to have been warped by the fact that I didn't buy them new clothes. As far as I know, they have turned out to be very well-adjusted human beings and haven't had to go in for counseling to deal with the fact that their mom didn't buy them new school clothes.

It goes back to that old fear thing again, that our kids will be laughed at in school and they will blame us and hate us for the rest of our lives.

Two things I have learned about kids:

First, if they feel loved and accepted at home, then peer pressure doesn't affect them nearly as much as it affects kids who aren't loved.

Second, **children's attitudes are usually direct copies of their parents'**. So if not having name brand clothes and new school clothes doesn't bother the parents, then the kids will pick up that attitude. Don't make a big issue out of things, not just in your actions but also in how you think, and your kids won't either.

If your children do need some things, like underwear and socks or shoes, then the beginning of the school year is the time to buy these things because stores have some great sales on them.

When possible give children clothing they need for Christmas and birthdays. That doesn't mean that is all the kids should get, but have grandparents or yourself give them maybe half toys and half clothes. You can even make it a family tradition, like giving all the kids a new pair of matching p.j.s to wear on Christmas Eve. Or do what my mom does. She gives all the grandkids and great grandkids a pair of warm fuzzy socks with a little money tucked into them. They love it. We all love opening up her presents at the same time and then putting on our new fuzzy socks to wear the rest of the evening. **Lighten up. More things and more money spent doesn't automatically mean more joy and fun**.

The Low Down on Laundry Detergent

I grabbed the phone and answered it. It was my daughter chuckling on the other end. **"We got another one," she said, "another laundry detergent e-mail."** For years now we have had one recurring question. How can I save on my laundry detergent?

This may seem like an innocent enough question, but when we find out the writer's story, laundry detergent is almost never really relevant to the problem. What we've found is that a person who asks about laundry detergent is usually on the brink of bankruptcy, divorce, or losing a job. It's like some kind of code word or distress signal for "Help Me -- I'm drowning in debt."

Often these people have maxed out their credit cards, fully mortgaged a quarter of a million dollar home, and owe money on several expensive new cars. They have closets full of designer clothes, purses, and shoes, and they ask "How can I save on laundry detergent?"

For a person in this situation, asking that question makes as much sense as saying, **"My home is burning down -- I must go back in and save that $3 carton of milk I bought today!"** If it were me, I would say, "Forget the milk! I'm going to save the family heirlooms, my gold jewelry, and the good silver."

I have tried to understand why in a financial crisis so many people want to learn how to save money on laundry detergent when there are so many more obvious ways they could be saving money. Here is what I have finally concluded:

First, by focusing on a trivial issue, some people don't have to look at the real, more serious problem. It's like putting a Band-Aid on a scratch on your finger while you are bleeding profusely from an artery on your leg. They don't want to acknowledge the real spending problem because then they would have to deal with it.

If you are in this situation and you want to be free of it, **YOU HAVE TO FIRST ADMIT THERE IS A PROBLEM**. You are spending more money than you make. It is important to realize that spending impulsively beyond your means is almost as bad as doing drugs. You get instant gratification and pleasure but over the long haul, it will destroy you.

Second, saving on laundry detergent gets rid of that nagging guilt for a little while. As long as you keep trying to save pennies on unimportant things, you don't have to feel guilty about spending thousands on the fun things. The problem is that if you are spending beyond your means, it will catch up with you eventually, which will make the stress and damage all the worse.

For those of you who do have your finances under control and really do need a way to spend less on detergent, here are a few suggestions.

At first I wondered how I could help anyone save money on detergent when a person uses so little of it. For a family of four, a 40-load box of detergent would last me one to two months, which doesn't give a lot to save on.

I then had a light bulb moment! **It isn't the laundry detergent that people need to save on but the amount of**

laundry they are doing! It seems as if people's laundry has turned into some kind of monster that is taking over their homes. It's everywhere. Piles of laundry on the floor, chairs, tables, and beds. Almost every horizontal surface in the house is covered with laundry -- dirty laundry, clean laundry, and folded laundry.

By cutting back on the amount of laundry you do, you can save quite a bit of money on detergent, dryer sheets, fabric softener, and hot water.

Here are a few ways to help you cut back:

Have the kids wear the same pair of pajamas for more than one night. Before you get upset and say there is no way you would allow them to do that, think about this: you bathe your kids before they go to bed, so their pajamas go on a clean body. How dirty could those pajamas get while the kids are sleeping? Most people don't change their sheets more than once a week. What is the difference between sleeping on the same sheets and sleeping in the same pajamas?

Assign each person his or her own towel to use a minimum of two to three times instead of just once. In the case of young children, let them all use the same towel. Up to a certain age, most people toss their little ones in the bath together, so if they can share the same bath water, they can share the same towel. Also if the towels are hung up right away after they're used, instead of left lying on the bathroom floor, they'll stay cleaner longer.

When you get home from church or someplace where you didn't wear an outfit all day, **change out of your good clothes and hang them up to wear again.**

If it doesn't look dirty and doesn't stink, don't wash it. We usually wear the same pair of jeans for a week at our house.

Don't be lazy. So often we get undressed and, instead of putting our clothes away, we throw them on the floor in a heap. We don't want to iron, fold, or even hang them up, so we just throw them in the wash. This makes more work later because we still have to iron, fold, and hang them on wash day, but we also use more detergent, dryer sheets, fabric softener, hot water, and time.

Don't use your dryer. Not only do you save on electricity but wear and tear on your clothes. Where do you think all that lint is coming from that's in your lint trap?

If clothes are looking limp and tired, then spray them with spray starch or fabric sizing and iron them. If you can't afford the starch, then mist with water. Even the water helps things to look crisper.

Babies

Grandma Tatum, Grandma Bessie, Jill and baby Tawra

As much as we all would love to have a cute nursery and every new baby item on the market, they really aren't necessities.

Here are some baby items that I never had, and I survived without.

Crib - I kept my son in a bassinet until he was about six months old. My grandson was in just a fold-up playpen until he was over two. So you don't need a crib right away. When you do go to buy one, be sure to check garage sales or see if you have a friend or family member who has one. You can find new inexpensive cribs with all the safety features.

Changing table - I never did have one. But if you are lucky enough to get one, be sure and use it for other things when baby outgrows it. My daughter used hers forever as shelving to keep the kids clothes and toys on when they got older. I then used the table for a while just as shelving in my sewing room and then in the utility room. After that she took it back to use as a changing table for baby #3.

High chair - I did have one, but there were times when I couldn't use it, and I found that a car seat works just as well to sit your baby in to feed him/her. Just set it on the floor or table.

Wipes - When I had babies, wipes weren't invented yet. It really wasn't as bad as it seems. I used a roll of toilet paper to wipe the baby first and then used a damp warm washrag to wipe after the toilet paper. I would keep a special stack of washrags or rags for this purpose alone. When they were dirty, I just threw them in the wash with my diapers or the whites, and I would use bleach and then rinse a second time.

If I had a really bad diaper blow-out, then I would use a couple of damp paper towels.

When I had to go someplace, I kept a small roll of toilet paper in the diaper bag and then put a wet washrag in the diaper bag before I left the house. I still will throw a wet washrag into a sandwich bag when I take my grandkids for the day to wipe off hands and face. I personally like that better than wipes because they are not as slick as a wipe and tend to rub things off easier.

After the christening of his baby brother in church, Jason sobbed all the way home in the back seat of the car. His father asked him three times what was wrong.

Finally, the boy replied, "That preacher said he wanted us brought up in a Christian home, and I wanted to stay with you guys."

Toys

David and Tawra in their homemade playhouse made out of a stove box.

Tawra wearing her homemade Halloween costume.

Kids don't really need as many toys as you think. When I first became a grandma, of course, I wanted my grandkids to have every toy under the sun, but I quickly found out something interesting. They played with the same few things over and over and didn't really care about the "cool" stuff. Here are a few basics, and most can be purchased at thrift stores or garage sales:

Balls - all sizes

Baseball bat

Blocks - You could even use things like your plastic leftover containers. My mom had a box of Dixie cups, and my kids loved stacking them and building pyramids with them.

Jump rope

Games - checkers, Old Maid, cards, 1-2 board games like Sorry or Chinese checkers.

Coloring books and crayons - My kids don't even need those because they love to just draw with paper and pencil.

Things around the house.
Cool Whip containers and spoons for digging outside
Hose and sprinkler to play in the summer
Bucket of water and paint brush to "paint" pictures on the sidewalk
String with macaroni, buttons, or beads to make necklaces
Cardboard boxes of every size:

Appliance boxes for forts
Small boxes for doll beds
Medium boxes turned upside down for a tea table
Babies love to sit in boxes and be pushed around in them

Baby toys - The definition of a toy is something for a child to play with. To a baby or toddler, that includes anything and everything. Why do you think they love exploring everything? They can't tell the difference between the plastic cups, bowls, and spoons that they play with in the tub and the $15 tub toys you bought them. My grandkids have more fun with my empty detergent bottle and my kitchen funnel when they're in the tub than anything else. Babies love measuring spoons, wooden spoons, and empty spice bottles with buttons or beans inside to make them rattle. (Of course, tape it shut.) Look around your kitchen and you'll find all kinds of things.

To clean toys from yard sales:

Throw all the stuffed animals in the washer and dryer. This will clean and re-fluff them.

For hard surfaces wipe down with a solution of bleach water.

Things like ink markings on plastic doll faces will come off with a small amount of scrubbing with Comet or baking soda.

Some toys, such as teething rings and small plastic toys, can be thrown in the dishwasher or sterilized with bleach water.

Telltale signs of Advanced Parenthood...
(Author Unknown)

You count the sprinkles on each kid's cupcake to make sure they're equal.

For Moms only! You only have time to shave one leg at a time.

You hide in the bathroom just to get some "alone time."

You consider finger paint to be a controlled substance.

You've mastered the art of placing large amounts of scrambled eggs and pancakes on the same plate without anything "touching."

You hope ketchup is a vegetable because it's the only one your child eats.

You con your kid into thinking that "Toys R Us" is a toy MUSEUM and not really a store.

You fast-forward through the scene where Bambi's mom gets killed.

You hear YOUR parents voice when it's you that screams "Not in THOSE clothes you don't!"

and finally, you KNOW you're a victim of Advanced Parenthood when you start offering to cut up other people's food for them!

Teenagers

David, Jill and Tawra

I can hear you now. **All those ideas are great for young children, but I have <u>teenagers</u>!** So? I admit that there are times when teenagers seem like aliens from another planet, but deep down, they are just like any other human being, they need to be loved. If you have a good attitude about your situation then they will too. (Usually, we hope. ☺)

In some ways teens should be easier. They are old enough for you to sit down with them and say, "We have a problem. Your dad has lost his job, or your dad has left, or I was irresponsible and foolish with my money, and now I'm trying to fix things. I really need your help."

If you are sincere about changing and fixing things, your teens will pick up on it, and in most cases (if the parents have the right attitude) your teenagers will be more than **willing to help and work with you.**

Most kids and teens have a very strong sense of fairness and justice. They know that sometimes your financial problems are beyond your control. They are usually more than willing to pitch in and do what they can, even if it means they'll have to sacrifice some things, especially if they can sense your sincerity and willingness to change. That's the key to it all.

Sometimes teens may have to work to help with the household expenses. This really won't hurt them at all; if anything, it will give them a stronger character and sense of responsibility. Working will teach them good time management too because they have to learn how to get their homework done before they go to work. It also leaves very little time on their hands to get bored or into trouble.

Remember if your teens are willingly working hard to help you out, be sure to show them you appreciate them on a daily (hourly?) basis. Also, you know that sense of fairness and justice in them? Respect that and don't treat yourself to a day out with friends when they are leaving for work instead of going to a football game. You make sure you sacrifice as much, no, *more* than you are expecting your teen to.

I am not so naive to believe that all families are such that your teens are going to look at you with a great big smile and say, " Sure, mom and dad. I am more than willing to give up everything you have overindulged me in for the past 16 yrs.- No problem."

Just because you have had a revelation about your finances doesn't mean your teen has. Be as patient and understanding as you can, **but you must also be firm,** and when push comes to shove, *you* are the one in charge and that includes making decisions about money.

If they keep whining and throwing a fit about those new jeans or shoes they want, very lovingly but firmly say, "You may have them, but you will have to pay for them yourself." Then stand firm and don't cave. If your teens are acting like this, the chances are you are in your financial mess because you have over indulged yourself, and look where it got you. **If you want your children to learn from your mistakes so they won't have to suffer the stress you have been through,** then don't give into them now.

Teens are more than capable of paying for their extra expenses, such as cars, car insurance, movies, sports and equipment fees, and special food like sodas and junk food.

"Sometimes I lie awake at night, and I ask, 'Where have I gone wrong?' Then a voice says to me, 'This is going to take more than one night.'"

Charles Schulz "Good Grief, Charlie Brown!!"

Entertainment

**David and Tawra in their homemade wedding outfits
made out of bread bags and old curtains.**

I really didn't have much time or money for fun and entertainment. I didn't go to the movies or sporting events, have parties, or even go out for a cup of coffee with a friend. I couldn't go to most extra church activities because everything costs money, including the Bible studies.

Now as miserable as that all seems, it really wasn't that bad. I did get to do a lot of fun things.

I could:
Go to the park for a picnic
Play ball
Play Frisbee
Lay on the grass and read a book
Go see a parade
Hear a concert in the park
Build a snowman
Have a snowball fight
Have a friend over for a visit
Attend special events around town. For example, our zoo has "dollar days" several times a year

There were lots of things to do at the library:
Read those magazines I couldn't afford to buy
Check out videos or DVD's
Just be able to sit and read a book in silence

They even have lots of entertainment events there like:
Puppet shows
Story time for the kids
Movies and classes for adults.

My husband and I once didn't have money for a date, so we went and parked in the far corner of the Wal-Mart parking lot and just sat and talked. It was one of our most fun times. Spending time alone talking with your spouse can help a marriage much more than spending money together.

I always made sure I had one day of rest. Usually it was Sunday. That in itself was wonderful to me to just have an entire day to do nothing.

Cheap Entertainment

Stare at people through the tines of a fork and pretend they are in jail.

Pay your electric bill in pennies

Mail yourself an anonymous love letter

Eating Out

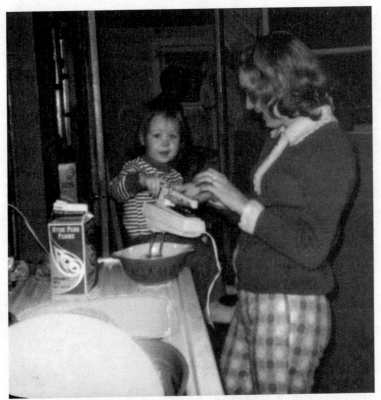

Jill trying to teach Tawra to cook

I didn't go out to eat at all. No fast food, no pizzas, not even an ice cream cone or can of pop. Sometimes for a special occasion like a birthday, we would go get ice cream, but even then, we wouldn't get the largest sundae or milkshake they had-- just a small cone.

When things do start getting under control, you can then start going out to eat. Here are a few tips to help.

Use coupons and ad specials when you can.

Eat out only for special occasions--birthdays, anniversaries, etc. Then work up to eating out maybe once a month as your income grows.

You don't need to go to really expensive restaurants. It may be that you can only afford fast food places for awhile.

No matter where you go, don't let your eyes get bigger than your stomach. Everything can look so good that you go crazy ordering. Don't order more than you can comfortably eat. Sometimes feeding everyone a light snack before you leave can take the edge off your hunger and you won't be tempted to buy as much.

Try not to buy the most expensive thing on the menu just because you want it. Start looking at their specials or the less expensive items.

Split your meals. Usually you get way too much to eat for one order anyway. In the case of small children, buy one hamburger and split it between them. If they eat that and still want more, then you can buy more food.

Always drink water and never buy dessert. If the dessert is something you really want, then order a small meal and make your dessert the main part of your meal.

Order appetizers in place of a full meal. They are usually less expensive and just the right amount.

Ask if you can order off the children's or senior citizens' menus. Some places also have half orders. Even if they don't show it on the menus, ask if they have them.

If a waiter asks if you want this or that with your food, don't be embarrassed to ask if it is included with the meal. Some of those little extra expenses, like cheese and sour cream, can really add up.

Instead of going out for an entire meal for a special treat, just go out for dessert. My husband and I would do this a lot when just the two of us went out. We would go someplace and order two cups of coffee and a dessert to split.

Don't go to places where you have to pay a tip. Sometimes the tip can be as much as what I would pay for a full meal at a fast food place.

Home Improvement

David helping tear down the walls for the remodeling

Learn as many basic skills as you can. Home improvement centers give free classes on all kinds of things. Ask a friend, neighbor, or family member to show you how to do things.

Most people are usually very glad to show you how to do something that they are good at. How do you feel when someone comes to you and asks for your advice or to teach them something. Doesn't it make you feel good and proud that you can do something for someone else to help them? So give someone else a chance to feel that way too.

We have a wonderful resource that doesn't get used as much as it should and that is the older generation. Not only does teaching you make them still feel needed and useful (which they very much are), but **you can gain a wealth of knowledge without having to learn the hard way.** I once had an older neighbor who showed me how to do all kinds of things from canning to how to plant a lawn.

Another good resource for learning things is your public library, county extension, and of course the internet.

Some basic skills that you need to know are: sewing, using hand tools, making home repairs, changing the oil in your car, changing a tire or the air filter, etc.

Don't say I can't do that. I went from not knowing what a pair of pliers was to hanging pictures, putting in new toilets, laying carpet, and changing faucets. If something inexpensive stops working, my motto is if I can't use it anyway, what will it hurt to try and fix it.

I found that you can paint most everything. I learned you can mix your own paint too. I was able to buy cheap mis-mix paints at hardware stores or even free paint from the Hazardous Waste Recycling Center. It was basic art. If I needed purple and I only had blue and red, then I would mix them until I got the shade I needed. If I had dark blue and needed light blue, then I poured in some white.

Before they had the Home and Garden Network or Martha Stewart, **I painted linoleum floors, kitchen countertops, bathroom tiles, storm doors, and hardwood floors.** I had an old metal sink in my kitchen that my dad spray painted for me, and it looked like new. I think I was the first person in the world to paint over paneling and wallpaper. People said I was crazy and that it would never work, but it did and now years later everyone is doing it.

I once got free paint to paint the outside of my house, but when it was finished, the metal storm door was an awful eyesore. This was years ago when everyone said there is no way latex paint would stick to metal. **No one ever dreamed of painting a storm door. You just replaced them.** I thought, what do I have to lose? It couldn't look any worse, and if it didn't work, then I could replace the door, but if it did work, then I will have saved a lot of money. I painted the door and it worked. It changed the whole look of the house, and 25 years later it still has the paint on it.

When it came to floors, I learned that in small areas, I didn't need a carpet layer to lay carpet. I cut the piece of carpet to size, laid it down with a little bit of double-sided tape and it worked fine. I could sand, stain, and refinish a wood floor myself or in some cases just paint it.

There is one added bonus to successfully fixing something

yourself--a sense of pride and feeling good about yourself. You don't need to read every book in the library on self-esteem. Just get up and fix something once in a while, and it will accomplish the same thing.

This generation has more knowledge at their fingertips and easily accessible information than any other generation before them, but all the knowledge in the world (which we can have through the internet) is worthless if we don't use it. If something is broken, find out how to fix it and then do it.

1st rule of intelligent tinkering - save all the parts.

Decorating

David and Tawra in the painted living room. Jill painted
the walls a bright orange to distract from the fact that
the walls were crumbling.

I spent many hours in my home because I had my business there so I always tried to have it look as nice as I could. I tried to keep things stylish and nice. **I made do with what I had or what I could find that was inexpensive.** These are just a few ideas to get you started.

Watch decorating shows or flip through magazines to get ideas of how you could copy an updated look for less money.

I used sheets as curtains or tablecloths.

I used tablecloths for curtains.

I found a white shower curtain for a dollar at the Dollar store, using some pretty ribbon for curtain rings to hang it.

I made a duvet cover out of two white sheets I had. I then hand-sewed a crocheted tablecloth to the top of it for a very elegant look.

I had an ugly old picture frame that I spray painted, and it looked like new.

I got a piece of fur on sale at the fabric store for $5 and made a throw, throw pillow, and rug for my bedroom.

I bought end tables for $1 at a garage sale. I took legs off of a table with a bad top and added them to another board, screwed the legs on that board, painted it, and voila--a new table.

When I was making new curtains for my grandson's bedroom, if I had used the novelty fabric that he wanted, it would have cost $10 to make them. Instead I used a sheet that my daughter had bought for $1 and 2/3 of a yard of the novelty fabric. I used the black sheet for the body of the curtain and then just added a 9" band of the novelty fabric across the bottom. The whole thing cost me $2.50 instead of $10.00.

I do this with throw pillows too. If I find a fabric that I really love, I will buy a piece just big enough for the front of the pillow and use a scrap that I already have for the back, or buy something less expensive.

Throw pillows are the easiest way to change the look of a room, and you don't even have to know how to sew. Just take a square of material, wrap it around the pillow, pin or tie it in the back, and you have a whole new look.

If you have a favorite sweater, or your kids have a favorite T-shirt, you can't wear any more but hate to give up, then put an old throw pillow in it or stuff it. Sew or use fusible hem tap to close the neck. Fold the sleeves and hem to the back and pin or sew. You now have a cute pillow.

Twin sheets make great curtains. They come in so many colors and don't need to be hemmed or anything. You can kick them up a notch by adding trim or pretty tie backs. In homes with 8-10 ft. ceilings, place your curtain rod at the top of the wall by the ceiling to hang your sheets. This really makes an impressive and dramatic effect.

Create your own if you can't afford something. Once I needed some tie backs for my curtains, and I had to be able to pull the curtain back and let it down on a regular basis. I couldn't find anything less then $5, plus they didn't look all that great and I needed 16 of them. You do the math. $80 was a lot of money for just tie backs; as a matter of fact, they would have cost more than my curtains.

I came home very frustrated one day from shopping, still trying to figure out what to do for tie backs. The electrician had been working on my house and had left 10 inch scraps of heavy duty electrical wire all over. I was walking around picking up these scraps and bending them back and forth not paying attention to what I was doing. I was thinking about my tie backs. Then all of a sudden I looked at the electrical wire and had a light bulb moment.

The wire would be perfect for a tie back. I bent it in a u-shape, slipped a small sleeve of fabric on it, and nailed it to the wall. They worked great. They were flexible yet strong enough to hold their shape. It wasn't a case of "I was so clever--it was a case of "I was so desperate."

Recently my daughter and I redecorated my granddaughter's bedroom. Here are a few of the good deals we got:

We found a net canopy for $5 in perfect shape. This same thing I had seen at Bed, Bath and Beyond for $50 not too long ago. This worked great not only for a canopy but also for a headboard on her bed.

We also found a beautiful silk looking dust ruffle to match the quilt we were using for $2.28.

I walked into a store that had their Christmas things on sale, and they had large sage green and gold tassels for 12 cents each. I had looked at smaller ones that weren't nearly as nice for $5 at Wal-Mart.

I made 3 throw pillows that only cost me $1.00 for stuffing and 50 cents for some satin roses to put on them.

My granddaughter wanted her bed to be very high, so my daughter (and son-in-law) set the mattress on top of some of the kazillion boxes of cookbooks we are having to store for the business. With the dust ruffle on no one knows any difference.

We found a nice full-length mirror in a black frame for $5.

For a writing and coloring table, we used a table my daughter had picked up for free off the curb and just threw a frilly tablecloth over it.

For end tables we used more boxes of books covered with fabric.

For curtains we folded a round table cloth in half and placed it over the rod laying silk flowers across the top.

As I was going through my material to use, I ran across 2 pillow cases someone had given me along with a stack of material. They were the perfect color to go with my granddaughter's quilt. To make them look more like designer linens, I added a bunch of lace around the hems.

Why ask Why?

Why does someone believe you when you say there are four billion stars, but check when you say the paint is wet?

Furniture and Appliances

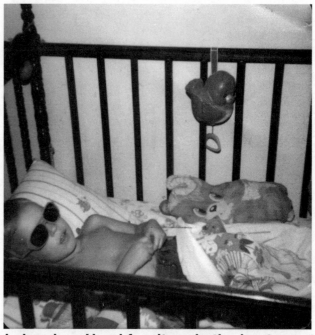

David sleeping. Used furniture is the best way to go when on a tight budget.

Only buy the absolute necessities. Even then you will be surprised with what you can do without. Most people would assume that a refrigerator is a necessity, but I have gone all winter without one, storing my things in the garage or outside in a cooler. Because the temperatures were below freezing, it kept everything just fine.

I also have done without a stove for a long time, using an electric frying pan, hot plate, and crock pot.

There really are very few pieces of furniture you can't do without in a pinch, but when I do have to buy something, I check out garage sales and thrift stores first. I found a very nice computer desk on the curb with a free sign on it. My daughter was expecting her first baby and needed a rocker. Shortly before the baby was born, she found a brand new one sitting by a dumpster.

Chest of drawers can be very expensive, and if you move as often as we do, they can be expensive and bulky to move. You can find a cheaper solution. For example, they have really nice canvas hanging shelves that could be used in place of a more expensive chest. At the moment I am using some small shelving in the bottom of my closet to stack all my sweaters, p.j.'s, etc., on.

You can find a lot of furniture that is so ugly that people will almost give it to you for nothing to take it off of their hands. Amazing things can then be done with a little bit of paint, new handles, or knobs.

Rusty old metal furniture can be spray painted and given new life.

Old chairs can be re-glued then painted or stained. If they are really ugly but sturdy, then just slipcover them. You don't even have to sew. I had an ugly chair and didn't have time to paint it, so I took an old lace curtain and threw it over the chair. I bunched it at the back, secured it with a safety pin, and hid the pin with a small bunch of flowers. I could have used a pretty brooch to pin it with if I hadn't had the flowers.

If you don't have a headboard for your bed, that's okay. There is nothing written in stone that says you have to have a headboard, and even if there was, it's still okay not to have one. But if you do want a head- board but don't have the money to buy one right now, then here are a few other things to try.

You can place the head of your bed in front of your windows and have your curtains be a backdrop.

Hang a large picture above your bed or make a collage of special smaller framed pictures.

Paint something behind your bed. It could be something as simple as squares. Don't be afraid to do this because if it doesn't turn out, you can always paint over it. It wouldn't be like you have to repaint the entire room.

My daughter has a shelf running around the center of her wall in her bedroom. It would be impossible to use a normal headboard. So she grabbed an old decorative door her brother was throwing out, polished it up, turned it sideways, and she had the perfect size headboard that she needed.

If nothing else, place several large pillows at the head of the bed. You wouldn't even have to always buy these. My daughter had these gigantic pillows that came with her couch but were uncomfortable to use there. She could have covered them to place on her bed. You could even save those old dead flat pillows you sleep on and put 2 of them together and cover. Just look around and see what you have.

It's just a matter of keeping your eyes and ears open and making do with you have. So often people will say, "But I'm not creative like you." Well, I don't have a creative bone in my body, but I do want to have a nice home, so that forces me to figure out how to get what I want or need by using what I have or can find for almost nothing; otherwise, I'll have to do without. That is a strong incentive for me to figure something out.

As I sit here alone in my sewing room/office,, I look around and am amazed at how little I paid for the furniture in here. I'm typing at a small computer desk that I found sitting on the curb with a free sign on it. I'm using my grandchildren's old changing table to spread out my paperwork and reference materials. It's even nicer than a long table because it takes up less space.

I have a sewing table, which is my most expensive piece in the room. I paid $10 for the table and 2 chairs many years ago and used it forever as a dining table, and now it is my sewing table. I have a bed down here for guests that I got for free from my son, who was getting rid of it to get a bigger bed for my grandson.

I could go on and on but really don't have the room to.

The main thing is to start looking around. Look in magazines, on TV, even at other people's homes and see what you like. Then go home, look around, and see how you can create the same thing with what you already have.

More Ways to Handle Stress

Mail a large letter using only one cent stamps.

Drive to work in reverse

Make up a language and ask people for directions.

Bill your doctor for time spent in the waiting room.

Utilities

Tawra and David in their winter bedrooms. We shut off
the entire house and only heated 3 rooms in the winter
to save on utilities. Each winter, our bedroom was the
family room.

As I sit here writing this, it is January in Kansas. The temperature dropped to 20 degrees last night, but **I didn't have my heat turned on all night.** It is now 11:30 am and I still haven't turned the heat on. I'm starting to feel a little cool (the temp. in the house is 50 degrees), so I will probably do one of two things.

Since I'm sitting in one place writing, I could turn on the space heater for a bit to take the chill off, or I will kick my heat on until the temp gets up to 60 degrees and turn it off then until this evening. I do the same type of thing in the summer.

Keep your thermostat at 78-82 degrees in the summer, 60-65 degrees in the winter.

Cool and heat only a couple of rooms and block the rest of the house off by shutting doors or covering doorways with blankets and closing vents.

At certain times of the year, we lived in only three rooms of my 2500 sq ft house. It was the kitchen, family room, and sewing room plus a small bathroom. We slept on the couch and floors. Since the sink we used to wash our face and brush our teeth was in the "cold" part of the house, my kids did not dawdle getting ready for school. There is always an upside to everything.

Make your home look cooler or warmer. In the summer pack away knickknacks and heavy wool rugs and throws. Put away anything that looks warm. Similarly, in the winter bring out things to add warmth. Keep lots of throws and blankets about. When people are cold, they can grab a blanket to wrap up in., This is cheaper than turning on the heat.

Move down to the coolest part or up to the warmest part of the house. In the summer move all your beds and/or the TV down to the basement. In the winter your upstairs room maybe the warmest so move up there.

Heat

Use a wood burning stove -- even if you have to have one installed. It will save you enough money that first winter to pay for itself.

Never buy wood for it. I would see that someone had cut down a tree and ask if I could have the wood. I cut up old pallets or skids. I went to a millworks, carpentry shops, or home improvement centers and asked for their scraps. The scraps didn't burn as long as logs, but so what if I had to check the fire more often. It was free.

Don't be afraid to ask. People were glad for me to haul this stuff off for them 100% of the time. I didn't have a pick up and had to haul everything in the back of my car ,so don't let not having a truck keep you from using your wood stove. Just put a tarp or old blanket down to protect your trunk.

Put plastic on your windows in the winter.

Wear layers during the winter so you can turn the heat way down. If the kids' feet are cold, have them put on socks and slippers. Don't just turn up the heat.

Place towels or blankets across bottom of doors or any

place where cold air is coming in.

Air Conditioning

In the summer open windows in the opposite corners of the house to "draw' the air through first thing in the morning. Then close them later before the heat of the day hits.

I did things where I was up and moving around (dusting, vacuuming, cleaning the bathroom) during the coolest part of the day.

Do the things that are less physical and more stationary (washing dishes, folding clothes, paying bills) in front of a fan during the hotter part of the day.

Use fans instead of central air or even air conditioners.

Put fans in your windows backwards to draw hot air out.

Use attic fans to draw hot air out too. Don't underestimate how much an attic fan can help. It can literally drop your home's temperature several degrees.

Water

Don't take 30+ minute showers.

I have timed it many times, and the adult human body can easily be washed from head to toe in 5 minutes. If you need to shave your legs, then add another 5 minutes, but at least try to cut back on shaving them to every other day.

I have a feeling that most husbands would rather have prickly legs once in a while then to have an emotionally prickly wife because she is stressed from finances.

Don't turn the water on for your shower until you are standing in it.

I know it's much nicer to let the water run to get warm before you get in, but sorry, you have to give up some creature comforts for a while. Remember just to be glad you have a shower and warm water.

There have been times I have not had hot water and have had to heat pans of water on the stove to carry to the tub for our baths. Trust me, after you have to do something like that, you aren't too picky and definitely don't grumble anymore.

Stop taking showers every day. If you just can't stand it and think you will die of armpit and crotch rot in one day (excuse me for being indelicate), then use a washrag and take a "sailorman's bath."

I'm sorry to sound like a broken record, but my biggest worry was how am I going to keep my children warm and fed today.

Actually in my pre-survival mode days, I thought cleanliness was next to godliness. **My babies usually had no less then 2 baths a day.** Then my son developed horrible rashes and sores on him. My dermatologist had a fit and said to stop bathing the baby so much. He had eczema, and bathing him that often was drying out his skin and making the eczema worse. He said I could only bathe him once a week. I could give him "spit" baths (where I wipe him with a wash rag), but that was all.

Stop taking baths. Filling up the tub takes 2-3 times more water than taking a quick shower. If you have babies and toddlers who can't take showers, then don't fill the bathtub too full of water. It's safer for them anyway. Better yet, toss in two or three kids at the same time.

Don't leave water running. When I brush my teeth, I wet my toothbrush, turn off the water, brush my teeth, and then turn the water on again to rinse. I do the same thing when washing my face. Wet the washrag, turn off the water, wash, then water on again to rinse.

Keep your hot water heater turned down as low as possible, around 120 degrees. It's safer for the children besides saving you money.

If you're worried about the water not being hot enough to kill germs, then don't worry about it. Most home water heaters can't get hot enough to really kill germs. Water needs to be boiling to kill all germs. That's why when we sterilize something, we put it in boiling water. If you need something sterilized, then add a small amount of bleach to the water to kill germs and bacteria.

Don't water the lawn. If you must water it, let the kids play in the sprinkler only when it's watering the lawn.

Why ask Why?

In winter why do we try to keep the house as warm as it was in summer when we complained about the heat?

Gardens and Yards

Tawra and David taking a break from yard work to enjoy
a wagon ride.

I pretty much couldn't have a yard, and what yard **I did have was what horticulturalists call xeriscape or native landscaping.** In other words, I had mostly weeds and anything that could survive with no water, fertilizer, or insecticide.

I had this idea that by living in Kansas, which is called "the grasslands," I might actually have some grass growing in the yard. Wrong! My husband always said that mowing our yard made as much sense as giving a bald man a haircut.

Joking aside, I would have loved having flowers and a great yard, but I didn't have the money to spend on annuals, fertilizers, water, or shrubs and trees. I did learn a few tricks, however:

Pouring boiling water or vinegar on weeds worked great to kill them. I did this on places like my driveway or sidewalk.

I learned gardeners are some of the kindest people around and are usually more than willing to share starts of plants or seeds from their flowers.

My daughter taught me that you can get free mulch from the city and by stopping and asking people or companies who are cutting down trees along the road. Most tree companies would be happy to dump the chips at your house, instead of paying to dump them at the recycle center or city dump.

I learned that compost piles are a must. Great fertilizer for the garden.

The county extension is a great free service to get all kinds of gardening advice.

Check the clearance section in your garden center for plants. I found enough plants to do the entire front of my house for $2.00. They were only ten cents each!

I knew I had reached the point where it didn't take much to make me happy, or I was very desperate when I started enjoying the cute purple flowers in my yard that were really weeds. **Plus beauty is in the eye of the beholder.** Ask any child under the age of five, and they will tell you that dandelions are beautiful yellow flowers. See, it's all in the way you look at it.

Cars

David and Tawra in their homemade horse and buggy

I never buy a new car. I've done the figures, and even with a great warranty, it is still less expensive to own a used car. Most warranties don't cover everything, and you find that the dealerships are no dummies. Usually what is not covered on the warranties is what will go out the quickest.

I found that even if I had to replace the entire engine on my car, it was still much cheaper than buying a new car.

Don't let poor self-esteem, the need to impress others, and an "I want that" mentality talk you into buying a new car.

Don't forget! **Another thing that can eat you alive with a new car is tags,** sales tax, and insurance. For some reason, people don't add those expenses in when considering whether to buy a new car or not, and it can be a huge on going expense.

There is one thing too about **owning a used car and that is less stress.** I never worried if my car got scratched, damaged, or in an accident. I never worried about it getting stolen because most thieves wouldn't be interested in my clunkers.

See if you can't make do without a car. Walk or take a bus when you can. Ride a bike. If you only use a car about 5 times a week, it could be cheaper to take a taxi than paying for all the car expenses like gas, maintenance, tags, and insurance. Don't make the mistake one of our clients did. She paid $3000 to have her car repaired in one big chunk. You can ride the bus or take an awful lot of cab rides for $3000.

What I Did For Emergencies

We dressed in layers to save on utilities.

Emergencies happen, and they can be even more frightening or frustrating when you have no extra money or credit cards to fall back on. You can survive them, though. I was not a person who dealt with emergencies well, but I found out like everything else that the more you have to deal with something, the easier it becomes and less frightening.

I'm talking about non-life threatening emergencies, like your fridge goes out or your car breaks down. I have learned how to fix most things or do without. Let me give you some examples. Like with everything else, you may say that there is no way that a person can do that, but you can, and I have in most cases.

These are things I did until I could save up enough money to fix or buy what I needed.

Your hot water heater goes out. I had to heat hot water on the stove for everything including baths. I could only do my laundry in cold water.

Your roof is leaking like a sieve. You just have to use buckets and pans and keep mopping up. Then, pray like crazy that it won't rain. I even had mine leak so badly that I had to put a child's swimming pool in the attic to catch all the water. It ruined the brand new sheet rock on my living room ceiling, and at times it would soak my bedding and mattress. I had to deal with this for about 10 years. This is one of those examples of being careful what you pray for; I had prayed for patience, and living with a leaky roof for 10 years certainly teaches you patience.

In most emergencies that I had, they were so far out of my control that I could do nothing but depend on God. I don't want that to sound trite or to make light of it because basically that is what happened. This was the case with my roof. After an exceptionally bad hailstorm, I went out to look at my roof and the damage. At this point I think I had more shingles on the ground than on my roof.

A man who owned several rentals on my street saw me out surveying my mess and walked down to say "hi." He said that my insurance company might pay for the damage but not to get my hopes up because 9 times out of 10 they didn't, but that it might be worth a try. So I called them.

The adjuster came and said, sure, they would cover it. Not only would they cover the roof, but they would pay for all the damage inside that the leaks had caused. New paint, new carpet, new sheet rock and even a new roof for my detached garage that was barely standing. I was so excited I was beside myself, and then he said, "You only need to come up with $1000 -$2000 to pay for the decking and deductible," and they would pay for the rest.

Talk about your bubble bursting real fast. I couldn't come up with $10 if my life depended on it, let alone $1000. I told the adjuster thank you and that I really couldn't afford it. He said that he would go back to the office and work out the numbers anyway, in case I could figure something out.

He seemed to be a very brusque man and I started to get discouraged, but instantly God brought to my mind the story of Nehemiah when he was going to ask the king if he could go to Jerusalem. Nehemiah asked God to soften the king's heart and to have the king show him favor. So all I could think to do was to pray that God would soften this adjuster's heart as he left. I didn't think any more about it because I knew there was nothing more I could do.

The next morning the adjuster called and said "I took your numbers home with me last night and did some figuring. If you can paint the rooms yourself and not put a roof on the garage (we couldn't roof it anyway because it was ready to collapse), then you could take the money for that and pay for the decking, so it won't cost you a penny."

Within a couple of weeks, I not only had a new roof but I had $2000 left over because I did a lot of the work myself on the inside of the house.

A few more common emergencies—

Your dryer goes out. Rig up a clothesline in the house or outside. Use a clothes rack. A lot of things you can hang on hangers to dry on your shower rod. It may not be the easiest way if you do a lot of laundry, but it can be done. Cut back on your laundry as much as possible.

Your lawn mower dies. Have funeral services and get out the hand clippers or better yet, rent a goat. Just "kidding" (no pun intended!).

I stopped watering the grass so it wouldn't grow as quickly, plus I did have to break down and borrow a mower from my neighbor. Most neighbors don't mind helping out in a case like this. I tried not to make a habit of always borrowing things because when a real need comes up, they didn't mind lending something to me like a mower. I also made sure I filled it with gas and sent it back in as good shape or better than when I borrowed it.

Getting help when my lawn mower died is another one of those cases of God intervening for me. It was Sunday after church and I went out on my front steps to sit. My yard was a mess. My lawn mover had been broken for a couple of weeks, and my grass looked awful. It had been one of a string of discouraging things that had happened, and even though it wasn't a major thing, it was like the straw that broke the camel's back. So I did what any red-blooded American woman would do. I started crying.

I sobbed and cried then prayed then sobbed and cried some more. Who would have thought that after all I had been through, a little overgrown grass would be my undoing. I felt like Elijah who had spent all that time defeating the false prophets and seeing miracles, and the very next day found him cowering in the desert running from Jezebel.

I pulled myself together and went in the house. I hadn't even been in there 5 minutes and I heard a lawn mower running. I wondered what in the world that noise was and ran out into the front yard. There was that same neighbor who owned the rental houses, and he was mowing my yard. He said he thought something must be wrong and I needed help because I usually kept my yard so nice. I explained about my lawn mower, and he insisted that I use his whenever I needed it. He even showed me where he kept the mower.

I do believe that man must have been an angel sent from God for me. Would you believe that I only saw him 3 times in the 25 years that I lived there? The first time was when my husband and I met him. He said he didn't live in our neighborhood but had rentals there. The second was when he told me how to get help with the roof, and the third time was with the lawn mower. It seemed I only saw him when I had a need.

Little (big?) things that go wrong with your car.

The heater goes out in your car. Use blankets and bundle up. It may even mean wearing boots and double socks to drive to work.

My car was in an accident, and the right fender had gotten bent such that if I turned the steering wheel to the right, it would badly scrape the tire. This meant that everywhere I went, I had to always turn to the left. I had to carefully map out where I was going before I left home; otherwise, I would be in a pickle.

This same accident had left the driver's door unusable, and I had to put plastic on the window. I couldn't use any drive thru anything. **To add to the mix, it was one of the coldest and snowiest January's** on record, so my battery would never work. Each morning I would have to get out and jump my battery before I could start my "left turn only" drive to work. Now that I think about it, I'm not sure why I even bothered with that car. It might have been easier to walk despite below freezing temperatures!

The moral of the story is… that you don't need to have a spirit of fear. Most emergencies work themselves out, and even though it may not be easy and is uncomfortable, **you have to learn to make do** or do without until you can afford to make repairs.

How to Make Do When You Don't Have Any Money.

Jill's first vacation in 20 years. She stayed with family in Oregon.

How to Make Do When You Don't Have Any Money

One way to save is for you to cut down on the number of items on your shopping lists and learn how to make do with what you have.

I get asked so often for *specifics* on how I saved money. There is nothing more frustrating than to go hear a speaker or read a book on "self improvement" things, and they spend the whole time telling you <u>why</u> you shouldn't do what you are doing and never <u>how to stop</u> what you are doing and how to change. So I thought it might help some of you to see what I did when I had a nice long shopping list but no money to spend. Before I start, though, there are a few general things I need to make clear.

1. All the lists our readers sent were exceptionally good and very hard to improve upon when it came to being careful and saving money. They bought only necessities and off brands when possible. They also knew that a lot of times you can get things for less at places like Dollar General, Dollar Tree, etc., and even at times places like Target had certain things for less. So when I say shopping list, I really just mean your shopping list for things other than food.

2. Some of the suggestions I make may seem very extreme and even hard to imagine anyone doing, but you have to keep in mind that there were times when I maybe had $3 and I would have to choose whether I was going to buy food for my children or Q-tips. What choice would you make? I really could not worry whether something was

109

politically correct, environmentally safe, or whether it was the acceptable and common thing to do. We had to eat, and I only had enough money for that at times. So keep that in mind when you read some of the "different" ideas that I came up with.

Actually, a lot of these ideas aren't mine--they come from generations of people who were very good at making do with what they had. It is hard for us to understand that there were times in our history when things like paper products were rare and very expensive. Such things as notebook paper, Kleenex, paper napkins and even toilet paper were not only expensive but also hard to come by. So people had to make do.

At times, I had to do the same thing, so I used some old-fashioned ideas and learned to make do.

3. Remember I didn't do these things forever, only for a short period, and only as the need arose. When I had the money, then I went back to buying things normally. I didn't buy excessively and I was still a wise steward, but when I had the money, I bought things that made my life a little easier.

4. Some of these tips are for people who are in dire straits right now, but for you others, you might find them helpful for those times when you just can't make it to the store for one reason or another.

5. Start looking at your shopping or grocery list in a different light. Do I really need this or that, or could I substitute something for it? Could I maybe make do without it for a week or two and wait until I will have the extra money?

PLEASE, PLEASE, PLEASE don't think I am saying that any of you should not be buying these things on your list. I'm not. I buy and have bought all of these things myself at some time. I'm just using these items as examples of what you might do if for some reason you can't buy them.

I won't be dealing with every item on the lists just because it would take too much time. There are also some things I won't deal with like feminine products. Sorry, but even I in my great wisdom (ha! ha!) have not come up with a good substitute for *those*! Ok, just so I don't get a ton of email, you can make and re-use your own but I will let you find the pattern on the internet. Plus, I won't deal with school supplies because I have touched on those in other articles.

One last thing. remember to take the ideas you can use and leave the rest. If you need a special lotion because your body will break out into hives if you use something else, then of course you can't substitute baby oil for your special lotion.   Or if you work as a hand model for a company advertising hand lotion, then you probably will need to buy rubber gloves to keep your hands nice, whereas a normal person could probably make do without them for a while. I can't possibly know every person's situation, so I will be talking in generalities.

Let me begin with an example of one of my shopping lists. I arrived at the discount store and had forgotten to bring my extra money. I had no checkbook and didn't want to use my credit card. I had only $7 in my wallet. Here's how I decided what I should buy.

Weed killer
    I needed to kill some weeds on my driveway and sidewalk,

so I decided that I could use vinegar or boiling water instead of much more expensive brand-name weed killers. I could even break down and hand-pull those weeds.

Remote for TV

This was a no-brainer. Would it really kill me to have to get up and turn the channels manually for a bit-- especially since I didn't have cable with 1001 stations?

Lotion

I could use some baby oil I had. I put it on in the shower so it isn't as greasy.

Rubber gloves

Since I don't use rubber gloves all the time, I could pull the plastic gloves out of that box of hair color that I had at home and use them for a while.

Scotch tape

I had masking tape and a glue stick at home. Wouldn't those work in most cases when I needed tape?

Small frying pan

I had a large frying pan I could use for the moment. Also where's the law that says I can't fry some things in a medium sauce pan?

Panty Hose, neutral

I had plenty of black panty hose but no neutral. Guess I will just have to wear outfits that I can use my black panty hose with.

Dishwasher Detergent

This was a no-brainer. I had plenty of liquid hand washing

detergent so guess I will just be hand washing my dishes again. I never had a dishwasher (unless you count my kids) until the last 3 years so I think I could manage to hand wash them for a bit.

As you can see, I ended up not really "having" to buy anything on the list.

Here are some ways to "make do" from those great lists that our readers sent me:

Batteries
I would swap batteries from one thing to another. I would take the batteries out of my kids' toys and put them in the TV remote. If I was totally out of batteries, then often I just couldn't use the battery operated item until I could afford to buy batteries.

Air freshener
Boil some water on the stove with a little cinnamon, ginger, and cloves sprinkled in it. Of course, lighting candles or even just plain old -fashioned opening the windows works too.

Ammonia
If you are using it for different cleaning uses, other than getting rid of a wax build up on a floor, then you probably have some other cleaning product in the house that you can use in place of it. If you were using it for cleaning as a disinfectant, then you could replace it with alcohol, hydrogen peroxide, or Clorox. If used as a degreaser, then Dow bathroom cleaner or just some good old hot soapy water and a scrubby pad often works just fine.

Antifreeze

There isn't a lot to substitute for antifreeze but check your recycling center because a lot of times they will have some antifreeze there.

Baby Powder

I love baby powder and the way it smells, but when I didn't have the money for it, I used cornstarch.

Bactine

Most medical items are a must, but you could use hydrogen peroxide in a pinch.

Baggies - small

You can use plastic wrap, aluminum foil, wax paper, and in a real pinch, the waxed bag that cereal comes in.

Baking soda

If using for cooking, then you may have to just not use recipes that call for it. If used for cleaning, then replace it with other cleaning supplies you have (see ammonia). If used in the fridge for odor, try using a couple pieces of charcoal.

Bath wash

If need be, you may have to use just regular mild bar soap. If you have a baby in the house, buy something like Ivory soap, and you will kill two birds with one stone--soap for you and the baby.

Bias tape

Can make your own out of fabric

Birth control
Aaaaaaaa, what can I say to this one? Give your hubby a kiss and sleep in twin beds for the next 30 years. Just joking.

Borax
Vinegar used as a rinse can also help brighten clothes and make them softer.

Burp cloths
You can use almost anything for a burp cloth -- cloth diaper, cotton dish towel, receiving blanket. In the case of Tawra's baby girl, we had to use bath towels and regular blankets to catch everything. I made all these cute burp cloths when my kids were born, but I found out real fast there never seemed to be one around when I needed it, so I was always frantically grabbing for anything I could find.

Carpet Deodorizer
You can use baking soda instead.

Cleaners for kitchen, bath, windows, floor
The reality of any cleaners is that hot soapy water cleans most everything. If you need the area to be sanitized, then use a few drops of Clorox in the water. Hydrogen peroxide or alcohol can be used as a disinfectant too.
If you are cleaning a surface that doesn't need to be disinfected, such as a window or mirror, then just plain water will work. Use a slightly dampened rag to wipe the surface and then go over it with a dry lint-free cloth.
The main thing to remember when using soap and water or any other cleaner is to always dry the area. This helps get rid of any water spots that might be left.

Clorox wipes

Sometimes when you are short of money, you have to give up conveniences, and this is a perfect example. As handy as these wipes and many others are, they are basically a paper towel or rag with cleaner of some sort sprayed on them. In the case of Clorox wipes, just fill an 8 oz. bottle with water and 4-5 drops (truly that is all you need) of Clorox and spray on a rag, or you can spray on the surface and let it set for a minute or two and then wipe.

Coffee filters

Use a paper towel that has been cut down.

Conditioner

Vinegar works really well. If you need shampoo too, you might try using a shampoo and conditioner in one. For years when we had a hard rain, I would run out to get my hair wet or put a bowl out to catch some rainwater. It makes your hair very soft.

Cotton Balls and cotton squares

I have never bought a cotton ball before. I don't use them that often. If you use them to remove nail polish, use some toilet paper instead. For taking off make up, use toilet paper or a washcloth that you save for that purpose only. I do save the cotton that comes in some medicine bottles for those rare occasions when I need a cotton ball.

Deodorant

I was so glad to see that everyone's list had deodorant and other personal hygiene products on it. I and the rest of the world thank you! HA! HA! In a bind, though, baking soda works really well.

Dish Soap
I have used laundry detergent before although you have to be a little careful because it makes the dishes a little slippery. In a real bind, you can wash them in very hot water and then dip them in some water with a little Clorox in it.

Dishcloths for washing dishes
Use old wash rags or cut up rags

Drano
If your drain is just sluggish, sometimes sprinkling some baking soda down it and then pouring vinegar on top will help. Let that set for a couple of minutes and then top it all with a kettle of boiling water. I even just recently had a sluggish bathtub drain and as a last resort used the plunger on it. It worked. Why didn't I think of that sooner? Duh? It even cleared up the sink drain in the kitchen at the same time.

Dryer Sheets
I love using dryer sheets and fabric softener, but when things are tight, your clothes will come clean without them.

Fabric softener
Vinegar will rinse every bit of soap out and helps soften the clothes.

Febreeze
Baking soda or a bowl of charcoal placed in a closet will absorb the smell.

Floor Cleaner
See bathroom and kitchen cleaners above

Kleenex
Use toilet paper.

Leaf bags
If you are using them for leaves, then just run your lawn mower over the leaves instead of raking them. If you rake them, find a corner in your yard where you can dump them and let them decompose.

Light bulbs
When I couldn't get light bulbs, I would take one out of a lamp or some place that wasn't used very often and put it where I needed it the most.

Limeaway
If you are using it for mineral build up, then it can be replaced with vinegar. If you are using it for rust, then just cover the surface with lemon juice and sprinkle with salt. In each of these cases, let it set for a bit before wiping off.

Notepad
I know paper is cheap, cheap, cheap, but I still hate to waste it. I cut up scratch paper into the size I want and staple them in the corner. This gives me several nice little note pads. If your kids are just scribbling and coloring, have them use the back of old homework papers. If they have to figure math problems, have them use old scratch papers for that too. When you are scribbling a note to other members of the family, use the back of scratch paper.
Definition of scratch paper: any paper that has been used on only one side and is no longer needed.

Mouthwash
I got this tip from a reader and it works great. Swish your

mouth with 1/2 hydrogen peroxide and 1/2 water. An added bonus is that it really whitens your teeth too.

Music CD's
I could never seem to have extra money for music, so I just always listened to the radio.

Napkins
Paper towels or small hand towels

Notebook paper
You can't substitute anything for paper, but be sure that you don't waste the paper you do have. See notepad pg.118.

Nursing pads
You can cut up a disposable diaper into small squares. Be sure to put the waterproof side towards your bra.

Paper Towel
Rags. Cut up those old flannel pj's, cotton T shirts, towels, and washrags.

Pet food, treats, and supplies
Of course, you can't really do without food for your pets, but here are a couple of things that might help. There may be times when you don't have the money to buy a large bag of pet food, so even though it is a little more per pound, you can buy a smaller bag and then maybe next time have enough money to buy a larger bag where you'll get more for your money.

There was a time when I fed my dog rice with a couple of tablespoons of hamburger in it for a week. I had tons of rice, so it was cheaper for me to do that. I knew it wouldn't hurt my dog because over the years the vet had recommended that I feed my dog that every once in awhile to get his digestive system back on track.

Treats of course are just that and not necessary. Remember, I'm not saying don't ever give your dog treats. This is just an idea if you need to cut back on this particular shopping list.

Picture frame
Think out of the box on this one. I don't know how many times I have covered a piece of cardboard with fabric and stuck a picture into the center of it. I add buttons, rick rack, and ribbon around the edges--anything that maybe matches the theme of the picture. You could almost think of it as scrapbooking but just using one picture.

If this is too complicated for you, then you might try what I have hanging in my hall right now. It's a display of family pictures without one frame used. At one point the whole extended family dressed in black with blue jeans, and we all had our pictures taken. Because everyone was dressed the same and the color was the same, the grouping of these pictures work really well. Most people get excited enough over the pictures that they don't even notice that I don't have them in frames.

I even saw the other day where someone took an old window that had several panes in it and put a picture in the center of each pane and hung it on the wall.

Plastic containers for storage
Use cardboard boxes, especially ones like banana or apple boxes that you can get at the grocery store, or go to a printer for boxes that paper comes in.

Prescriptions
Of course you can't substitute these, but be sure and check at Wal-Mart or Target, etc. to see if your prescriptions are one of the ones you can get for $4.

Q-tips
You can use a small piece of toilet paper carefully rolled around a bobby pin. Or check around for good prices on generic Q-tips. Just last week I bought a bag of 1000 generic Q tips) for 50 cents at Walgreens. You can get great buys sometimes in unexpected places.

School uniform shirts, pants
We just got a great tip from one of our readers, Mary Beth. She didn't have the money for new school uniforms, so she took the old uniform pants and cut off the pant legs for her kids to wear as shorts and cut the long sleeves on their shirts for short sleeve shirts. That way she can make do for those first couple of months of school. It also helps to spread the expense of school supplies and uniforms out a little bit.

Stamps
I didn't find this out for years, but my grocery store had special mailboxes for all my main utilities. I just put my bill in its envelope with no stamp and put it in its mailbox. It may not seem like much, but some months I would have only 3 stamps left, so I could then use those for my house payment and other bills.

Staples
You can use paper clips and in some cases just turn the page corner down.

Toilet Cleaner

Clorox, denture cleaner, or often I just sprinkle in Comet and it does a great job.

Toothbrushes
Years ago they used to wrap a rag around their finger and use baking soda or salt to brush their teeth. I tell you this not so you won't buy toothbrushes but in case you ever find yourselves in a pinch without one, you will know what to do.

Toothpaste
Baking soda or salt

Trash can
If it is a trash can for rooms other than the kitchen, you can use many different things. Buckets, tall narrow baskets, and right now I have an antique enamel "slop" bucket that I am using in my office. Even a cardboard box will do in a pinch. When I say the sky's the limit, that's exactly what I mean.

Vinegar, white
If you are using it for cooking, then there is no substitute. But for cleaning, then you can check the cleaners list above to give you some hints.

Watch
I have worn a watch since I was 10 years old and didn't think I could function without one. My daughter, on the other hand, has never been able to wear a watch because they short circuit when she puts one on. I didn't know how she managed without one. (Now she has 3 clocks in every room!) About 8 months ago my watch died on me, and I haven't replaced it yet. I couldn't believe it, but it hasn't been too bad living without it.

In conclusion, I didn't deal with some things like hair

color, nail polish, pocket knives, gift bags, hair clips, and paper plates because these are things that I think most of us know we could do without if we had to. I also didn't touch on any over –the-counter meds because most of these, like food, are necessities.

There were a lot of toiletries and things like bug spray on the list, so here is something that maybe you all didn't know about. I don't usually send in many rebates but there are two that I do on a regular basis -- Walgreen's and Ace Hardware. I have not had to buy shampoo, conditioner, body wash, toothbrushes, toothpaste, mouthwash or make up for 3 years. Walgreens has some great things like this on their rebates each month. The items are totally free with the rebate. It's a great deal!

Ace rebates are great too. They usually have a good rebate sale at each holiday like Memorial Day, Fourth of July, Labor Day, etc. If you sign up for an Ace awards card (no obligation and doesn't cost a thing), they will send you a flyer in the mail when they are getting ready for a rebate sale.

From their rebates I get things like bug spray (to kill bugs in and out of your house and to spray on you to keep them away), weed killer, Dow bathroom cleaner, dish detergent, work gloves, Murphy's oil, black cloth to keep the weeds out in your flower bed, drill bits, saw blades, glues, and much much more. So you might check into these.

Miscellaneous Money Savers

Jill made her dress for her church Valentine's banquet.

You don't need cable TV.

You don't need a cell phone. I have even gone without having a phone at all for awhile.

Stop your newspaper and magazine subscriptions.

Stop buying expensive gifts for everyone. That doesn't mean you have to stop giving at all, but instead, give of your time or yourself or perhaps give something less expensive but with special meaning.

Start looking for things at garage sales. I find things all the time in unopened packages that are brand new to give. My daughter-in-law loves Thomas Kinkaid puzzles. I found one brand new for 75 cents that I gave her for Christmas. Did that make the puzzle any less good or mean that I love my daughter-in-law any less? Of course not.

Some of the most unusual gifts and ones my children loved the most have been one-of-a-kind things that I have bought used. What I find amusing is that one place everyone loves to go to now (even Martha Stewart) is e-bay. What is it? Nothing but the biggest garage sale in the whole wide world, so get over that stigma of buying things used.

Use what you have. My granddaughters needed Bible covers, so I took more old fur and made them one. My grandmother-in-law gave me for Christmas one time a set of pillow cases that she had crocheted when she was first married. They had no real monetary value, but they were priceless to me.

You may not get much praise from others for being a wise steward (I mean I have never once had a family member come up to me and say, "Thank you, Mom, for getting my shampoo for 50% off"), but you can always know that God is pleased with you for doing your best and for me that is praise enough. Plus, it can be fun to watch your money go further.

Garage Sales

Tawra and David riding around in the front yard.

10 Garage Sale Shortcuts

1. There are two kinds of garage sales – the ones where people want to make money and the ones where people want to get rid of stuff. The object is to find the ones where people want to get rid of stuff.

2. Get a map and newspaper and map out your route. Photocopying maps from a phone book works great. Using this method, you can easily visit 25 sales an hour. If you're a beginner, you might hit neighborhoods you are familiar with first.

3. If at all possible, leave the kids at home. If you must take them, use a baby backpack or an umbrella stroller to make it easier. Give older children 25 or 50 cents and let them see what good deals they can get. Kids love picking out gifts for grandparents, siblings, parents, and other family members, and bargain hunting helps them learn about money. Bring snacks (animal crackers, cereals, crackers in a plastic bag works well) and cold water for everyone, and plan ahead for potty breaks. If you have children with you, it's best to plan on hitting only about five sales until you see how they do.

4. Wear cool, comfortable clothes. Bring lots of change and one dollar bills. Put your money in your pockets so you don't have to worry about carrying your purse. Also bring a tote bag to carry your finds as you walk.

5. When you find something you're not sure you want, pick it up and carry it around while you continue looking. Otherwise, someone else may take it while you're trying to decide.

6. Always ask politely if they will come down on the price. Most of the time they will. Every once in a while, some things are so reasonable that I do not feel right asking the seller to take less. Finding women's sweater's at $1 each isn't bad, but I still ask if they will take 50 or 75 cents. If I find a name brand sweater in perfect shape for 25 cents, I don't ask for less.

7. If there is something you really want, but the seller is asking more than you want to pay, offer them a lower price. If they say no, leave your name and number and ask them to consider selling it to you at your price if they still have it at the end of the day.

8. Always check items well for hard-to-see tears, stains, or breakage. Remember it is a garage sale, so everything won't be perfect.

9. It is best to go early, but don't panic if you can't. Sometimes you get the best buys after lunch when sellers are tired and don't want to have to drag everything back into the house. It's great to go on the last day of a sale because most sellers will almost pay you to take things so they don't have to keep them.

10. If you don't have success in one part of town, try somewhere else the next time. Sometimes the best garage sale neighborhoods are the ones you don't expect. Don't be embarrassed about buying at garage sales. Some of the wealthiest women in the world love garage sales -- Martha Stewart and Oprah are among them! When you're finished hunting for bargains, go home, put your feet up, and have a nice glass of ice cold lemonade. Grab the phone and call someone who will share the excitement and appreciate your good buys. Garage sales are like old fishing stories. Die-hards always brag about the one that got away!

How to have a garage sale

Your objective is to make money while getting rid of stuff in your house.

Here are some tips to make the most of your garage sale.

The spring is the best time to have a garage sale. After a long winter, people are ready to get out and find some good deals.

Clean out everything you can so you can have as large a sale as possible. If you don't have enough stuff to make a big enough sale, then ask friends, family, or neighbors to have one with you. Also give all of your neighbors a flyer telling them when you are having a sale and ask if they would like to have one also. The more sales in one area, the more people will come to your sale.

Check and see if any of your local papers or thrifty papers have free garage sale ads. Put one in if they do.

Signs

Have as many signs as possible. Put one on every major corner, on the corners of your street, and any needed in between. If it is more than ½ mile from the corner to your house, put some signs in between. You really cannot make too many signs. Make your signs LARGE--at least 12 inches, but 18-24 inches is much better. Make it with contrasting colors. Black and white are best, but other colors such as colored paper with black will work well. A black permanent marker works best.

Be sure to put your address AND an arrow pointing the direction to your house. Make your address in large readable letters and the word "sale" smaller, not the other way around. Make all your signs out of the same material. For example you could make all of them out of cardboard with white painting. That way, people will know it's your garage sale and recognize which signs to follow.

Don't forget to take them down when you're done!

Setting Up

Have things as neat and clean as possible.

Make things easy to look at. Don't have 10 cardboard appliance boxes, stuffed full of clothes, sitting around for everyone to dig through.

Spread your items out as much as possible or hang up your clothes. Try not to stack your clothes 3-4 ft. deep on your tables.

Keep like things together as much as possible. Kids things, including toys, in one area. Tools and lawn equipment in another. This may seem like a lot of work, but it really isn't if you just decide where each section is going to be beforehand and place the items in that area as you carry them out.

Set your tables out with good traffic flow in mind. If possible, arrange it so people can look from both sides of the tables.

Have a small table, even a TV tray will do, for a "pay" table. Keep a money box with lots of change, sacks, small cardboard boxes, black marker, pens, paper, and masking tape.

Pricing

Price your stuff LOW. There is nothing more frustrating than going to a garage sale and seeing items that you could buy brand new on clearance for the same price that they're marked at the sale. Name brands (like Baby Gap) can let you get by with a little higher prices. I would recommend pricing really nice kids clothes no higher than $1 each and clothes that have stains or are not name brand at .50 or less. Socks and underwear shouldn't be higher than .10 each. You may think that these prices are too low, but please remember than you are *getting rid of stuff!!* You don't want to bring it back into the house.

You will also get a lot more sales if your prices are reasonable, which means more total money in the long run. For example, if you sell 200 items at .25/ea, you'll make more money ($50) than if you keep your prices higher and sell only 15 of the items at $1/ea.

Be sure to put price stickers on everything. There is nothing more frustrating than to go to a garage sale and you have to ask about every little thing you want to buy. I usually don't stay at these sale very long. They take up twice as much time.

If you don't want to put an individual price on each and every item, then price things in groups. For example, make a large sign saying that all children's clothes are 50 cents unless otherwise marked, or all books are 25 cents unless otherwise marked, etc.

A good rule of thumb is to price items a maximum of 10% retail price.
By the way, people who go to yard sales really don't care if it's brand new in the box and you paid $80 for it so you "have" to get $50 for it. It has been sitting in your house for who-knows-how-long, so you aren't getting your money's worth anyway. Price it for $5 and get rid of it!

Expect people to ask you to come down on the price. If you feel your prices are very reasonable, then don't come down, but remember you are trying to get rid of stuff, so don't put too high a price on things.

If someone asks you to come down on a price and you aren't ready to at that point, ask for their name and number and tell them you will call them if it hasn't sold and you want to sell it to them at their price.

Garage Sale Misc.

Prepare snacks and meals that are easy to grab and eat the day before.

Have an extension cord or electrical outlet handy if someone needs to test something.

Smile and say "hello" as people walk up so they will know who to give the money to and they know you are watching them.

If you can, have a "free box" of odds and ends. So often if someone takes something out of the free box, they feel they should buy something too. More sales.

Working at Home

Tawra and David helping during the remodel. Jill worked at home on her piano business in the middle of a house that was torn apart.

If You Want to Work at Home, Be Creative!

Disclaimer: This section is for mom's who really want to stay at home with their children and feel that is what is best for their family. If working outside of the home is what works best for your family, then that's what you need to do for them.

You want to stay home with your children, but due to circumstances beyond your control, you are their sole support. What jobs can you do and still be at home for the kids? There are many magazines out there that have lists of stay-at-home jobs, but they don't seem to work out for a lot of individuals. I don't think they work for two reasons.

First, many people haven't really made up their minds that their children's emotional and spiritual needs are greater than their children's material wants. Being present in our children's lives is more important than buying them things.

When I made up my mind that the most important and best thing for my children was for me to be there for them, that became my main goal. Then when a job came along, I didn't consider the best job to be the one that paid the most, but the one that gave me the most time with my kids.

The second reason moms have trouble finding jobs that allow them to stay home is that each individual's circumstances, gifts or talents, and needs vary so greatly. It is difficult for anyone to suggest a handful of solutions that will work for everyone.

For example, at one point I was working at a very well paying receptionist job. When my daughter had a long term knee injury, however, I had to leave that job for a job that paid less because it gave me the freedom to pick her up at all different times of day. Another time when both my children were seriously ill and I couldn't leave them at all, I stayed home and ironed clothes for other people.

I became incredibly determined, like an Olympic swimmer or long distance runner, trying to achieve my goal. I got up early and worked long, hard days. I sacrificed much to obtain my goal. I overcame my natural shyness and told everyone I met that I ironed, baked cookies, built piano parts, or could do whatever they needed. I did that in order to find the work that I needed to achieve my goal--to be there for my kids.

There are times when I had to do jobs that I never dreamed I could do, that I knew nothing about, and that I really didn't *want* to do, but I had to overcome my fear and just do them anyway. One of those jobs was starting up my husband's business again.

At the time I was working at an interior decorating shop, sewing and making $4.50 an hour. Even back then, that was peanuts for wages. I was miserable working there. It was the first job that I got after my husband left, the first time I worked away from home.

It was in the dead of winter, and I had to leave for work just a little before my kids had to go to school. They were old enough to walk to school alone but not quite old enough that I trusted them not to lose the house key. I had nightmares of them losing the key and standing in below-zero temperatures

142

for an hour until I got home from work. There were no neighbors they could go to or call me from. Plus, they hated coming home to an empty house. They had gone from having both mom and dad at home all the time to having no one there. Then there were the days it was really too cold for them to walk to school, but I had no one I could ask to drive them. It was a pretty awful time.

After four months working there, I came home, and in the mail was a letter saying that the bank was going to foreclose on the house because of a lien from some past due business debts of my husband's. I had two weeks before I had to be out of the house. It was like something out of a melodrama, where the mean banker is going to take the poor widow's home and throw her out on the street, except that it was really happening to me.

I had been up against so many unbelievable things those past few months, but this was too much. After much crying, wailing, and gnashing of teeth, I finally calmed down enough to ask God what in the world was I supposed to do. I said, why can't I have a business at home? You know, some cute craft something or other, so I could be there for the kids. He very clearly said, "You *have* a business at home, and I want you to do it." When my husband left, he literally had left everything from the business.

Like most people do when they don't want to do what God has asked of them, I started in with the excuses. Number one, I didn't know anything at all about my husband's business. The business was building player pianos, nickelodeons, or calliopes, not my cute little craft shop. I had never used a drill, let alone a drill press, or even known what a lathe was, let alone how to use it.

Then there was the bank. How could I possibly even figure out how to make the products in two weeks, let alone get customers lined up and get the products made?

God told me to do 2 things. First, call our old production manager, which I thought would do me no good at all. I had no way of paying him, and he wasn't going to leave a high paying job to come and work for me for nothing. But I had learned years ago that no matter how unrealistic the odds were, if I obeyed God, it always turned out for my best, so I made the call.

He was so excited to hear from me and even more excited to hear that I wanted to start up the business again. "How about I work for 3 nights a week and all day Saturday?" he said. He also said he wanted to work for nothing! I wouldn't allow that, though, so he suggested that he work for extra products that I had stored away and wasn't using, instead of paying him in cash.

To say I was in shock by the time I hung the phone is an understatement. But it gets even better. I couldn't do the business if I didn't have a home to do it in. So as soon as I hung up, God had me do the second thing, much to my dismay, and that was to call the banker.

Now let's think about this. Like I'm going to call the banker and say "I'm starting up my husband's business pretty much from scratch, which I know nothing about. I have no money to pay, and don't know when I will have any, but will you let me keep my house?" Well, that's exactly what I did.

When I finished giving him my little speech and telling him what I had planned, he simply said "Fine." I could not believe it, so I repeated myself and said "You do realize I know nothing about doing this?" "I know," he said, "but I know you and I know you can do it, and when you can pay me, you will." He also said that he knew it would take me quite awhile to get up and going, so they would just defer payments until then, even if it took one or two years.

I started 2 days later on my "new" business. Oh, one other small detail I forgot to mention. My husband had made not only our customers but also our suppliers extremely mad at us. Moreover, we owed lots of money to these suppliers. The parts I needed I couldn't get just anywhere, so I couldn't just go to some other supplier. But God had literally worked a miracle for me, so I just took one obstacle at a time. As it turned out, in less than 6 months, I was making payments to the bank, and in about 5 years, I was successful enough to have paid off $35,000 in business debt.

Don't be afraid to try anything. Stop saying but I can't do this or I can't do that. **Most of all, stop making excuses.**

If you are stumped at what kinds of jobs or things you can do to stay at home and earn money, here are a few suggestions:

Think about things that are a little out of the ordinary. Don't do crafts!! You usually spend more time, money, and energy than you will ever earn. That's why they call them "starving" artists.

Try to think of needs that people need fulfilled. I did ironing and found out that I made more money doing that than I did working as a receptionist.

I had a woman who brought me her groceries, disposable pans, and her favorite recipes for me to **cook 15-20 of her favorite meals.** She would then store them in her freezer for the month. If you have extra garden produce, try selling it to the restaurants in your area. You can grow herbs very easily and restaurants love fresh herbs.

Don't limit yourself to only working "at home" if you can work at a job that still fits your need to be at home during certain hours of the day. And don't be afraid to ask for what you want. For example, if you would love to work in the school cafeteria because that job has the same hours that your children are in school, don't be afraid to ask if there is an opening. If you can sew, inquire at decorating shops. A lot of times they need seamstresses who can do basic sewing and work flexible part-time hours. A lot of businesses also need someone to run errands, and you can often adapt their hours to your needs.

I once found the perfect receptionist job for me that allowed me to be at home during the hours I needed to be home. I didn't want to leave for work until the kids had left for school, and I wanted to be home when they got home from school. Another time I went to a small baker , and she told me I could choose what hours I wanted to work. These types of jobs are out there. You just need to look.

If you're thinking, "but I have a degree and I must find a job in my area of expertise". You need to rethink things. Your main goal at this point is that you want to stay at home with your kids so if your degree is not providing you with a job that allows you to do that, you need to set it aside for the moment and stop using it as an excuse for not finding the right job. Remember, your education, high standard of living, and material things are not what is important at this period in your life -- raising your children is.

A customer you don't want!

A customer sent an order to a distributor for a large amount of goods totaling a great deal of money.

The distributor noticed that the previous bill hadn't been paid. The collections manager left a voice-mail for them saying, "We can't ship your new order until you pay for the last one."

The next day the collections manager received a collect phone call, "Please cancel the order. We can't wait that long."

Was it worth it?

Yes, it was hard physically and emotionally, but spiritually, there is no describing how good it was. When I did what was right, God blessed me.

You may say "Well, if He was blessing you, why didn't He give you more money, etc.?" We seem to forget or not understand that there are more parts to our world than just the physical or material. There's the spiritual part of us.

God knows what we need more of sometimes are *spiritual* blessings. However, because of our make up, it sometimes takes a few physical and emotional struggles before we are willing to accept those blessings.

In the amplified Bible, the definition of a blessing is to be inevitably fortunate and spiritually prosperous, happy with life--joy and satisfaction in God's favor, to be envied regardless of our outward circumstances.

Oddly enough, I was envied more during my most desperate financial times than at any other time. The most important part of the above definition, though, is that God will make you *spiritually* prosperous. I mean, really think about what it means to be prosperous or rich spiritually. I had peace, no stress, I was calm, and I had a clear mind to make wise decisions. Romans 14:17 (KJV) "For the kingdom of God is not meat and drink; but righteousness and peace and joy in the Holy Ghost. "

To most of us, being blessed does not mean being

spiritually prosperous but being given wealth, health, and perfect kids. We are like unwise little children who, when given a choice of what to order at a restaurant, would order only ice cream, cake, and pop for our meal. We can't understand why our parents won't let us have that but order salad, veggies, and milk instead. Being wiser, the parent knows that we children need the salad, etc., to help us grow, and after we eat a good nutritious meal, we can then have our dessert.

What good is an expensive home, car, or clothes if we have no peace and are so stressed out that we can't think straight half of the time? I'm so glad God is a wise parent and helps me to have a well-balanced life, who gives me dessert *after* a nutritious meal.

It didn't happen overnight. Trust me, I PMSed (I know that's not a word, but you get my point) with the best of them. There were moments when I wanted to holler, scream, and give in, but each time God was there to pull me up by my bootstraps when I couldn't deal with things myself.

He knew I was trying the best I could to show honor and integrity to Him, and He blessed me. He blessed me with exactly what I had been asking for--wisdom, love, peace, patience, and thanksgiving. Even more important, He blessed me with children who have grown up to love Him, who are responsible, and who have honor and a great sense of integrity-- children who are now teaching all these things to my grandchildren, the next generation. Does it get any better than that? You see, it really was worth all the hard work, and the dividends just keep multiplying.

Jill with her six grandkids in 2010. She found these stockings at the $1 store and filled them with goodies from garage sales, thrift stores, dollar stores and freebies for the kids for Christmas! Each filled stocking was less than $15.

Need a little inspiration to save money, get out of debt and get your home in order?

Keeping It Clean

This e-book series includes 3 e-books to help you **conquer the laundry pile, get your house in order and reduce your stress** with better organization.

Learn more at http://www.livingonadime.com/store

Penny Pinching Mama:
500 Ways I Lived On $500 A Month

As a single mother of two, best selling author **Jill Cooper started her own business without any capital and paid off $35,000 debt in 5 years on $1,000 a month income.**

In her book she shares how she did it! This book is filled with practical, everyday ideas to help anyone stretch a small income.

Learn more at http://www.livingonadime.com/store

To order online

Print Books:

Dining On A Dime Cookbook, Eat Better Spend Less
Menus From Dining On A Dime
Quick And Easy Menus On A Dime
Penny Pinching Mama
Dig Out Of Debt

E-Books:

Dining On A Dime Cookbook
Groceries On A Dime
Penny Pinching Mama
Dig Out Of Debt e-Book series
Menus On A Dime e-Book Series
Pretty for Pennies
Moving On A Dime
Gifts In A Jar
Saving With Kids e-Book Series
Valentine's Day On A Dime
Winning The Credit Card Game
Halloween On A Dime

**For online orders or free frugal tips and recipes
visit www.LivingOnADime.com**

Order Form

Please send me:

_ copies **Penny Pinching Mama** $12.95 ea $_____
_ copies **Dining On A Dime Cookbook** $19.95 ea $_____
_ copies **Menus From Dining On A Dime**

                                        $ 6.95 ea $_____

_ copies **Quick And Easy Menus On A Dime**

                                        $14.95 ea $_____

_ copies **Dig Out Of Debt** $17.95 ea $_____

Shipping & Handling **(US Only)** 1 book $ 4.50 $_____
                   each additional book $ 1.00 ea $_____
                                Subtotal $_____
Colorado Residents add 2.9 % Sales Tax $_____
                                    Total $_____

     * *Canadian Orders Triple Postage*

       Please enclose check payable to ***Living on A Dime.***

Ship To:

Name_____

Address_____Apt. #____

City_____ State ___Zip_____

Email Address_____ Phone_____

(Please include in case there is a problem with your order, We do not sell
our customers' email addresses or phone numbers)

Mail To:

Living On A Dime
P.O. Box 193
Mead, CO 80542

Credit card orders may be placed online at:
www.LivingOnADime.com

Order Form

Please send me:

_ copies **Penny Pinching Mama** $12.95 ea $_____

_ copies **Dining On A Dime Cookbook** $19.95 ea $_____

_ copies **Menus From Dining On A Dime**
                             $ 6.95 ea $_____

_ copies **Quick And Easy Menus On A Dime**
                            $14.95 ea $_____

_ copies **Dig Out Of Debt** $17.95 ea $_____

Shipping & Handling **(US Only)** 1 book $ 4.50 $_____

                each additional book $ 1.00 ea $_____

                        Subtotal $_____

Colorado Residents add 2.9 % Sales Tax $_____

                          Total $_____

   * *Canadian Orders Triple Postage*

Please enclose check payable to ***Living on A Dime.***

Ship To:

Name_____

Address_____Apt. #___

City_____ State ___ Zip_____

Email Address_____ Phone_____

(Please include in case there is a problem with your order, We do not sell
our customers' email addresses or phone numbers)

Mail To:
Living On A Dime
P.O. Box 193
Mead, CO 80542

Credit card orders may be placed online at:
www.LivingOnADime.com

Order Form

Please send me:

_ copies **Penny Pinching Mama** $12.95 ea $_____

_ copies **Dining On A Dime Cookbook** $19.95 ea $_____

_ copies **Menus From Dining On A Dime**

                         $ 6.95 ea $_____

_ copies **Quick And Easy Menus On A Dime**

                         $14.95 ea $_____

_ copies **Dig Out Of Debt** $17.95 ea $_____

Shipping & Handling **(US Only)**1 book $ 4.50 $_____

            each additional book $ 1.00 ea $_____

                         Subtotal $_____

Colorado Residents add 2.9 % Sales Tax $_____

                              Total $_____

   * *Canadian Orders Triple Postage*

      Please enclose check payable to *Living on A Dime.*

Ship To:

Name_____

Address_____Apt. #____

City_____State ___Zip_____

Email Address_____ Phone_____

(Please include in case there is a problem with your order, We do not sell
our customers' email addresses or phone numbers)

Mail To:

Living On A Dime
P.O. Box 193
Mead, CO 80542

Credit card orders may be placed online at:
www.LivingOnADime.com